FREEDOM IN KANSAS.

SPEECH

OF

WILLIAM H. SEWARD,

IN THE SENATE OF THE UNITED STATES,

MARCH 3, 1858.

WASHINGTON.
BUELL & BLANCHARD, PRINTERS.
STEREOTYPE EDITION.
1858.

SPEECH OF MR. SEWARD.

Mr. PRESIDENT: Eight years ago, we slew the Wilmot Proviso in the Senate Chamber, and buried it with triumphal demonstrations under the floors of the Capitol. Four years later, we exploded altogether the time-honored system of governing the Territories by Federal rules and regulations, and published and proclaimed in its stead a new gospel of popular sovereignty, whose ways, like those of wisdom, were to be ways of pleasantness, and all of whose paths were supposed to be flowery paths of peace. Nevertheless, the question whether there shall be Slavery or no Slavery in the Territories, is again the stirring passage of the day. The restless Proviso has burst the cerements of the grave, and, striking hands here in our very presence with the gentle spirit of popular sovereignty run mad, is seen raging freely in our halls, scattering dismay among the Administration benches in both Houses of Congress. Thus an old and unwelcome lesson is read to us anew. The question of Slavery in the Federal Territories, which are the nurseries of future States, independently of all its moral and humane elements, involves a dynastical struggle of two antagonistical systems, the labor of slaves and the labor of freemen, for mastery in the Federal Union. One of these systems partakes of an aristocratic character; the other is purely democratic. Each one of the existing States has staked, or it will ultimately stake, not only its internal welfare, but also its influence in the Federal councils, on the decision of that contest. Such a struggle is not to be arrested, quelled, or reconciled, by temporary expedients or compromises.

Mr. President, I always engage reluctantly in these discussions, which awaken passion just in the degree that their importance demands the impartial umpirage of reason. This reluctance deepens now, when I look around me, and count the able contestants who have newly entered the lists on either side, and shadowy forms of many great and honored statesmen who once were eloquent in these disputes, but whose tongues have since become stringless instruments, rise up before me. It is, however, a maxim in military science, that in preparation for war, every one should think as if the last event depended on his counsel, and in every great battle each one should fight as if he were the only champion. The principle, perhaps is equally sound in political affairs. If it be possible, I shall perform my present duty in such a way as to wound no just sensibilities. I must, however, review the action of Presidents, Senates, and Congresses. I do indeed, with all my heart, reject the instruction given by the Italian master of political science, which teaches that all men are bad by nature, and that they will not fail to show this depravity whenever they have a fair opportunity. But jealousy of executive power is a high, practical virtue in Republics; and we shall find it hard to deny the justice of the character of free legislative bodies, which Charles James Fox drew, when he said that the British House of Commons, of which he was at the moment equally an ornament and an idol, like every other popular assembly, must be viewed as a mass of men capable of too much attachment and too much animosity, capable of being biased by weak and even wicked motives, and liable to be governed by ministerial influence, by caprice, and by corruption.

Mr. President, I propose to inquire, in the first place, why the question before us is attended by real or apparent dangers.

I think our apprehensions are in part due to the intrinsic importance of the transaction concerned. Whenever we add a new column to the Federal colonnade, we need to lay its foundations so firmly, to shape its shaft with such just proportions, to poise it with such exactness, and to adjust its connections with the existing structure so carefully, that instead of falling prematurely, and dragging other and venerable columns with it to the ground, it may stand erect forever, increasing the grandeur and the stability of the whole massive and imperial fabric. Still, the admission of a new State is not necessarily or even customarily attended by either embarrassments or alarms. We have already admitted eighteen new States without serious commotions, except in the cases of Missouri, Texas, and California. We are even now admitting two others, Minnesota and Oregon; and these transactions go on so smoothly, that only close observers are aware that we are thus consolidating our dominion on the shores of Lake Superior, and almost at the gates of the Arctic ocean.

It is manifest that the apprehended difficulties in the present case have some relation to the dispute concerning Slavery, which is raging within the Territory of Kansas. Yet it must be remembered that nine of the new States which have been admitted, expressly established Slavery, or tolerated it, and nine of them forbade it. The excitement, therefore, is due to peculiar circumstances. I think there are three of them, namely:

First. That whereas, in the beginning, the ascendency of the slave States was absolute, it is now being reversed.

Second. That whereas, heretofore, the National Government favored this change of balance from the slave States to the free States, it has now reversed this policy, and opposes the change.

Third. That national intervention in the Territories in favor of slave labor and slave States, is opposed to the natural, social, and moral developments of the Republic.

It seems almost unnecessary to demonstrate the first of these propositions. In the beginning, there were twelve slave States, and only one that was free. Now, six of those twelve have become free; and there are sixteen free States to fifteen slave States. If the three candidates now here, Kansas, Minnesota, and Oregon, shall be admitted as free States, then there will be nineteen free States to fifteen slave States. Originally, there were twenty-four Senators of slave States, and only two of a free State; now, there are thirty-two Senators of free States, and thirty of slave States. In the first Constitutional Congress, the slave States had fifty-seven Representatives, and the one free State had only eight; now, the free States have one hundred and forty-four Representatives, while the slave States have only ninety. These changes have happened in a period during which the slave States have almost uninterruptedly exercised paramount influence in the Government, and notwithstanding the Constitution itself has opposed well-known checks to the relative increase of representation of free States. I assume, therefore, the truth of my first proposition.

I suggested, sir, a second circumstance, namely: That whereas, in the earlier age of the Republic, the National Government favored this change, yet it has since altogether reversed that policy, and it now opposes the change. I do not claim that heretofore the National Government always, or even habitually, intervened in the Territories in favor of the free States, but only that such intervention preponderated. While Slavery existed in all of the States but one, at the beginning, yet it was far less intense in the Northern than in some of the Southern States. All of the former contemplated an early emancipation. The fathers seem not to have anticipated an enlargement of the national territory. Consequently, they expected that all the new States to be thereafter admitted would be organized upon subdivisions of the then existing States, or upon divisions of the then existing national domain. That domain lay behind the thirteen States, and stretched from the Lakes to the Gulf, and was bounded westward by the Mississippi. It was naturally divided by the Ohio river, and the Northwest Territory and the Southwest Territory were organized on that division. It was foreseen, even then, that the new States to be admitted would ultimately overbalance the thirteen original ones. They were, however, mainly to be yet planted and matured in the desert, with the agency of human labor.

The fathers knew only of two kinds of labor, the same which now exist among ourselves—namely, the labor of African slaves and the labor of freemen. The former then predominated in this country, as it did throughout the continent. A confessed deficiency of slave labor could be supplied only by domestic increase, and by continuance of the then existing importation from Africa. The supply of free labor depended on domestic increase, and a voluntary immigration from Europe. Settlements, which had thus early taken on a free-labor character or a slave-labor character, were already maturing in those parts of old States which were to be ultimately detached and formed into new States. When new States of this class were organized, they were admitted promptly, either as free States or as slave States, without objection. Thus Vermont, a free State, was admitted in 1791; Kentucky, a slave State, in 1792; and Tennessee, also a slave State, in 1796. Five new States were contemplated to be erected in the Northwest Territory. Practically it was unoccupied, and therefore open to labor of either kind. The one kind or the other, in the absence of any anticipated emulation, would predominate, just as Congress should intervene to favor it. Congress intervened in favor of free labor. This, indeed, was an act of the Continental Congress, but it was confirmed by the first Constitutional Congress. The fathers simultaneously adopted three other measures of less direct intervention. First, they initiated in 1789, and completed in 1808, the absolute suppression of the African slave trade. Secondly, they organized systems of foreign commerce and navigation, which stimulated voluntary immigration from Europe. Thirdly, they established an easy, simple, and uniform process of naturalization. The change of the balance of power from the slave States to the free States, which we are now witnessing, is due chiefly to those four early measures of national intervention in favor of free labor. It would have taken place much sooner, if the borders of the Republic had remained unchanged. The purchase of Louisiana and the acquisition of Florida, however, were transactions resulting from high political necessities, in disregard of the question between free labor and slave labor. In admitting the new State of Louisiana, which was organized on the slave-labor settlement of New Orleans, Congress practiced the same neutrality which it had before exercised in the States of Kentucky and Tennessee. No serious dispute arose until 1819, when Missouri, organized within the former province of Louisiana, upon a slave-labor settlement in St. Louis, applied for admission as a slave State, and Arkansas was manifestly preparing to appear soon in the same character. The balance of power between the slave States and the free States was already reduced to an equilibrium, and the eleven free States had an equal representation with the eleven slave States in the Senate of the United States. The slave States unanimously insisted on an unqualified admission of Missouri. The free States, with less unanimity, demanded that the new State should renounce Slavery. The controversy seemed to shake the Union to its foundations, and it was terminated by a compromise. Missouri was admitted as a slave State. Arkansas, rather by implication than by express agreement, was to be admitted, and it was afterwards admitted, as a slave State. On the other hand, Slavery was forever prohibited in all that part of the old province of Louisiana yet remaining unoccupied, which lay north of the parallel of 36° 30′ north latitude. The reservation for free labor included the immense region now known as the Territories of Kansas and Nebraska, and seemed ample for eight, ten, or more free States. The severity of the struggle and the conditions of the compromise indicated very plainly, however, that the vigor of national intervention in favor of free labor and free States was exhausted. Still, the existing statutes were adequate to secure an ultimate ascendency of the free States.

The policy of intervention in favor of slave labor and slave States began with the further removal of the borders of the Republic. I cheerfully admit that this policy has not been persistent or exclusive, and claim only that it has been and yet is predominant. I am not now to deplore the annexation of Texas. I remark simply that it was a bold measure, of doubtful constitutionality, distinctly adopted as an act of intervention in favor of slave labor, and made or intended to be made most effective by the stipulation that the new State of Texas may hereafter be divided and so reorganized as to constitute five slave States. This great act cast a long shadow before it—a shadow which perplexed the people of the free States. It was then that a feeble social movement, which aimed by moral persuasion at the manumission of slaves, gave place to political organizations, which have ever since gone on increasing in magnitude and energy, directed against a further extension of Slavery in the United States. The war between the United States and Mexico, and the acquisition of the Mexican provinces of New Mexico and Upper California, the fruits of that war, were so immediately and directly consequences of the annexation of Texas, that all of those transactions in fact may be regarded as constituting one act of intervention in favor of slave labor and slave States. The field of the strife between the two systems had become widely enlarged. Indeed, it was now continental. The amazing mineral wealth of California stimulated settlement there into a rapidity like that of vegetation. The Mexican laws which prevailed in the newly-acquired Territories dedicated them to free labor, and thus the astounding question arose for the first time, whether the United States of America, whose Constitution was based on the principle of the political equality of all men, would blight and curse with Slavery a conquered land which enjoyed universal Freedom. The slave States denied the obligation of these laws, and insisted on their abrogation. The free States maintained them, and demanded their confirmation through the enactment of the Wilmot Proviso. The slave States and the free States were yet in equilibrium. The controversy continued here two years. The settlers of the new Territories became impatient, and precipitated a solution of the question. They organized new free States in California and New Mexico. The Mormons also framed a Government in Utah. Congress, after a bewildering excitement, determined the matter by another compromise. It admitted California a free State, dismembered New Mexico, transferring a large district free from Slavery to Texas, whose laws carried Slavery over it, and subjected the residue to a Territorial Government, as it also subjected Utah, and stipulated that the future States to be organized in those Territories should be admitted either as free States or as slave States, as they should elect. I pass over the portions of this arrangement which did not bear directly on the point in conflict. The Federal Government presented this compromise to the people, as a comprehensive, final, and perpetual adjustment of all then existing and all future questions having any relation to the subject of Slavery within the Territories or elsewhere. The country accepted it with that proverbial facility which free States practice, when time brings on a stern conflict which popular passions provoke, and at a distance defy. This halcyon peace, however, had not ceased to be celebrated, when new-born necessities of trade, travel, and labor, required an opening of the region in the old province of Louisiana north of 36° 30′, which had been reserved in 1820, and dedicated to free labor and free States. The old question was revived in regard to that Territory, and took the narrow name of the Kansas question, just as the stream which Lake Superior discharges, now contracting itself into rivers and precipitating itself down rapids and cataracts, and now spreading out its waters into broad seas, assumes a new name with every change of form, but continues nevertheless the same majestic and irresistible flood under every change, increasing in depth and in volume until it loses itself in the all-absorbing ocean.

No one had ever said or even thought that the law of Freedom in this region could be repealed, impaired, or evaded. Its constitutionality had indeed been questioned at the time of its enactment; but this, with all other objections, had been surrendered as part of the compromise. It was regarded as bearing the sanction of the public faith, as it certainly had those of time and acquiescence. But the slaveholding people of Missouri looked across the border, into Kansas, and coveted the land. The slave States could not fail to sympathize with them. It seemed as if no organization of Government could be effected in the Territory. The Senator from Illinois [Mr. DOUGLAS] projected a scheme. Under his vigorous leading, Congress created two Territories—Nebraska and Kansas. The former (the more northern one) might, it was supposed, be settled without Slavery, and become a free State, or several free States. The latter (the southern one) was accessible to the slave States, bordered on one of them, and was regarded as containing a region inviting to slaveholders. So it might be settled by them, and become one or more slave States. Thus indirectly a further compromise might be effected, if the Missouri prohibition of 1820 should be abrogated. Congress abrogated it, with the special and effective co-operation of the President, and thus the National Government directly intervened in favor of slave labor. Loud remonstrances against the measure on the ground of its violation of the national faith were silenced by clamorous avowals of a discovery that Congress had never had any right to intervene in the Territories for or against Slavery, but that the citizens of the United States residing within a Territory had, like the people of every State, exclusive authority and jurisdiction over Slavery, as one of the domestic relations. The Kansas-Nebraska act only recognised and affirmed this right, as it was said. The theory was not indeed new, but a vagrant one, which had for some time gone about seeking among political parties the charity of adoption, under the name of Squatter Sovereignty. It was now brought to the font, and baptized with the more attractive appellation of Popular Sovereignty. It was idle for a time to say that, under the Missouri prohibition, freemen in the Territory had all the rights which freemen could desire — perfect freedom to do everything but establish Slavery. Popular Sovereignty offered the indulgence of a taste of the fruit of the tree of the knowledge of evil as well as of good—a more perfect freedom. Insomuch as the proposition seemed to come from a free State, the slave States could not resist its seductions, although sagacious men saw that they were delusive. Consequently, a small and ineffectual stream of slave labor was at once forced into Kansas, engineered by a large number of politicians, advocates at once of Slavery and of the Federal Administration, who proceeded with great haste to prepare the means so to carry the first elections as to obtain the laws necessary for the protection of Slavery. It is one thing, however, to expunge statutes from a national code, and quite another to subvert a national institution, even though it be only a monument of Freedom located in the desert. Nebraska was resigned to free labor without a struggle, and Kansas became a theatre of the first actual national conflict between slaveholding and free-labor immigrants, met face to face, to organize, through the machinery of republican action, a civil community.

The parties differed as widely in their appointments, conduct, and bearing, as in their principles. The free laborers came into the Territory with money, horses, cattle, implements, and engines, with energies concentrated by associations and strengthened by the recognition of some of the States. They marked out farms, and sites for mills, towns, and cities, and proceeded at once to build, to plough, and to sow. They proposed to debate, to discuss, to organize peacefully, and to vote, and to abide the canvass. The slave-labor party entered the Territory irregularly, staked out possessions, marked them, and then, in most instances, withdrew to the States from which they had come, to sell their new acquisitions, or to return and resume them, as circumstances should render one course or the other expedient. They left armed men in the Territory to keep watch and guard, and to summon external aid, either to vote or to fight, as should be found necessary. They were fortified by the favor of the Administration, and assumed to act with its authority. Intolerant of debate, and defiant, they hurried on the elections which were to be so perverted that an usurpation should be established. They rang out their summons when the appointed time came, and armed bands of partisans, from States near and remote, invaded and entered the Territory, with banners, ammunition, provisions, and forage, and encamped around the polls. They seized the ballot-boxes, replaced the judges of elections with partisans of their own, drove away their opponents, filled the boxes with as many votes as the exigencies demanded, and, leaving the results to be returned by reliable hands, they marched back again to their distant homes, to celebrate the conquest, and exult in the prospect of the establishment of Slavery upon the soil so long consecrated to Freedom. Thus, in a single day, they became parents of a State without affection for it, and childless again without bereavement. In this first hour of trial, the new system of popular sovereignty signally failed—failed because it is impossible to organize, by one single act, in one day, a community perfectly free, perfectly sovereign, and perfectly constituted, out of elements unassimilated, unarranged, and uncomposed. Free labor rightfully won the day. Slave labor wrested the victory to itself by fraud and violence. Instead of a free republican Government in the Territory, such as popular sovereignty had promised, there was then and thenceforth a hateful usurpation. This usurpation proceeded without delay and without compunction to disfranchise the people. It transferred the slave code of Missouri to Kansas, without stopping in all cases to substitute the name of the new Territory for that of the old State. It practically suspended popular elections for three years — the usurping Legislature assigning that term for its own members, while it committed all subordinate trusts to agents appointed by itself. It barred the courts and the juries to its adversaries by test oaths, and made it a crime to think what one pleased, and to write and print what one thought. It borrowed all the enginery of tyranny, but the torture, from the practice of the Stuarts. The party of free labor appealed to the Governor (Reeder) to correct the false election returns. He intervened, but ineffectually, and yet even for that intervention was denounced by the Administration organs, and, after long and unacceptable explanations, he was removed from office by the President. The new Governor (Shannon) sustained for a while the usurpation, but failed to effect the subjugation of the people, although he organized as a militia an armed partisan band of adventurers who had intruded themselves into the Territory to force Slavery upon the people. With the active co-operation of this band, the party of slave labor disarmed the Free State emigrants who had now learned the necessity of being prepared for self-defence, on the borders of the Territory, and on the distant roads and rivers which led into it. They destroyed a bridge that free-labor men used in their way to the seat of Government, sacked a hotel where they lodged, and broke up and cast into the river a press which was the organ of their cause.

The people of Kansas, thus deprived, not merely of self-government, but even of peace, tranquillity, and security, fell back on the inalienable revolutionary right of voluntary reorganization. They determined, however, with admirable temper, judgment, and loyalty, to conduct their proceedings for this purpose in deference and subordination to the authority of the Federal Union, and according to the line of safe precedents.

After due elections, open to all the inhabitants of the Territory, they organized provisionally a State Government at Topeka; and by the hands of provisional Senators, and a provisional Representative, they submitted their Constitution to Congress, and prayed to be admitted as a free State into the Federal Union. The Federal authorities lent no aid to this movement, but, on the contrary, the President and Senate contemptuously rejected it, and denounced it as treason, and all its actors and abettors as disloyal to the Union. An army was dispatched into the Territory, intended indeed to preserve peace, but at the same time to obey and sustain the usurpation. The provisional Legislature, which had met to confer, and to adopt further means to urge the prayers of the people upon Congress, were dispersed by the army, and the State officers provisionally elected, who had committed no criminal act, were arrested, indicted, and held in the Federal camp as State prisoners. Nevertheless, the people of Kansas did not acquiesce. The usurpation remained a barren authority, defied, derided, and despised.

A national election was now approaching. Excitement within and sympathies without the Territory must be allayed. Governor Shannon was removed, and Mr. Geary was appointed his successor. He exacted submission to the statutes of the usurpation, but promised equality in their administration. He induced a repeal of some of those statutes which were most obviously unconstitutional, and declared an amnesty for political offences. He persuaded the Legislature of the usurpation to ordain a call for a Convention at Lecompton, to form a Constitution, if the measure should be approved by a popular vote at an election to be held for that purpose. To vote at such an election was to recognise and tolerate the usurpation, as well as to submit to disfranchising laws, and to hazard a renewal of the frauds and violence by which the usurpation had been established. On no account would the Legislature agree that the projected Constitution should be submitted to the people, after it should have been perfected by the Convention. The refusal of this just measure, so necessary to the public security in case of surprise and fraud, was a confession of the purpose on the part of the usurpation to carry a Constitution into effect by surprise and fraud. The Governor insisted on this provision, and demanded of the President of the United States the removal of a partial and tyrannical judge. He failed to gain either measure, and incurred the displeasure of the usurpation by seeking them. He fled from the Territory. The Free State party stood aloof from the polls, and a canvass showed that some 2,300, less than a third of the people of the Territory, had sanctioned the call of a Convention, while the presence of the army alone held the Territory under a forced truce.

At this juncture, the new Federal Administration came in, under a President who had obtained success by the intervention at the polls of a third party—an ephemeral organization, built upon a foreign and frivolous issue, which had just strength enough and life enough to give to a Pro-Slavery party the aid required to produce that untoward result. The new President, under a show of moderation, masked a more effectual intervention than that of his predecessor, in favor of slave labor and a slave State. Before coming into office, he approached or was approached by the Supreme Court of the United States. On their docket was, through some chance or design, an action which an obscure negro man in Missouri had brought for his freedom against his reputed master. The Court had arrived at the conclusion, on solemn argument, that insomuch as this unfortunate negro had, through some ignorance or chicane in special pleading, admitted what could not have been proved, that he had descended from some African who had once been held in bondage, that therefore he was not, in view of the Constitution, a citizen of the United States, and therefore could not implead the reputed master in the Federal courts; and on this ground the Supreme Court were prepared to dismiss the action, for want of jurisdiction over the suitor's person. This decision, certainly as repugnant to the Declaration of Independence and to the spirit of the Constitution, as to the instincts of humanity, nevertheless would be one which would exhaust all the power of the tribunal, and exclude consideration of all other questions that had been raised upon the record. The counsel who had appeared for the negro had volunteered from motives of charity, and, ignorant of course of the disposition which was to be made of the cause, had argued that his client had been freed from Slavery by operation of the Missouri prohibition of 1820. The opposing counsel, paid by the defending slaveholder, had insisted, in reply, that that famous statute was unconstitutional. The mock debate had been heard in the Chamber of the Court in the basement of the Capitol, in the presence of the curious visiters at the seat of Government, whom the dullness of a judicial investigation could not disgust. The Court did not hesitate to please the incoming President, by seizing this extraneous and idle forensic discussion, and converting it into an occasion for pronouncing an opinion that the Missouri prohibition was void, and that, by force of the Constitution, Slavery existed, with all the elements of property in man over man, in all the Territories of the United States, paramount to any popular sovereignty within the Territories, and even to the authority of Congress itself.

In this ill-omened act, the Supreme Court forgot its own dignity, which had always been maintained with just judicial jealousy. They forgot that the province of a court is simply "*jus dicere*," and not at all "*jus dare*." They forgot, also, that one "foul sentence does more harm than many foul examples; for the last do but corrupt the stream, while the former corrupteth the fountain." And they and the President alike forgot that judicial usurpation is more odious and intolerable than any other among the manifold practices of tyranny.

The day of Inauguration came—the first one among all the celebrations of that great national pageant that was to be desecrated by a coalition between the Executive and Judicial departments, to undermine the National Legislature and the liberties of the people. The President, attended by the usual lengthened procession, arrived and took his seat on the portico. The Supreme Court attended him there, in robes which yet exacted public reverence. The people, unaware of the import of the whisperings carried on between the President and the Chief Justice, and imbued with veneration for both, filled the avenues and gardens far away as the eye could reach. The President addressed them in words as bland as those which the worst of all the Roman Emperors pronounced when he assumed the purple. He announced (vaguely, indeed, but with self-satisfaction) the forthcoming extra-judicial exposition of the Constitution, and pledged his submission to it as authoritative and final. The Chief Justice and his Associates remained silent. The Senate, too, were there—constitutional witnesses of the transfer of administration. They too were silent, although the promised usurpation was to subvert the authority over more than half of the empire which Congress had assumed contemporaneously with the birth of the nation, and had exercised without interruption for near seventy years. It cost the President, under the circumstances, little exercise of magnanimity now to promise to the people of Kansas, on whose neck he had, with the aid of the Supreme Court, hung the millstone of Slavery, a fair trial in their attempt to cast it off, and hurl it to the earth, when they should come to organize a State Government. Alas! that even this cheap promise, uttered under such great solemnities, was only made to be broken!

The pageant ended. On the 5th of March, the Judges, without even exchanging their silken robes for courtiers' gowns, paid their salutations to the President, in the Executive Palace. Doubtlessly the President received them as graciously as Charles the First did the Judges who had at his instance subverted the statutes of English Liberty. On the 6th of March, the Supreme Court dismissed the negro suitor, Dred Scott, to return to his bondage; and having thus disposed of that private action for an alleged private wrong, on the ground of want of jurisdiction in the case, they proceeded with amusing solemnity to pronounce the opinion, that if they had had such jurisdiction, still the unfortunate negro would have had to remain in bondage, unrelieved, because the Missouri prohibition violates rights of general property involved in Slavery, paramount to the authority of Congress. A few days later, copies of this opinion were multiplied by the Senate's press, and scattered in the name of the Senate broadcast over the land, and their publication has not yet been disowned by the Senate. Simultaneously, Dred Scott, who had played the hand of *dummy* in this interesting political game, unwittingly, yet to the complete satisfaction of his adversary, was voluntarily emancipated; and thus received from his master, as a reward, the freedom which the Court had denied him as a right.

The new President of the United States, having organized this formidable judicial battery at the Capitol, was now ready to begin his active demonstrations of intervention in the Territory. Here occurred, not a new want, but an old one revived—a Governor for Kansas. Robert J. Walker, born and reared in Pennsylvania, a free State, but long a citizen and resident of Mississippi, a slave State, eminent for talent and industry, devoted to the President and his party, plausible and persevering, untiring and efficient, seemed just the man to conduct the fraudulent inchoate proceedings of the projected Lecompton Convention to a conclusion, by dividing the friends of Free Labor in the Territory, or by casting upon them the responsibility of defeating their own favorite policy by impracticability and contumacy. He wanted for this purpose only an army and full command of the Executive exchequer of promises of favor and of threats of punishment. Frederick P. Stanton, of Tennessee, honorable and capable, of persuasive address, but honest ambition, was appointed his Secretary. The new agents soon found they had assumed a task that would tax all their energies and require all their adroitness. On the one side, the Slave-Labor party were determined to circumvent the people, and secure, through the Lecompton Convention, a slave State. On the other, the people were watchful, and determined not to be circumvented, and in no case to submit. Elections for delegates to that body were at hand. The Legislature had required a census and registry of voters to be made by authorities designated by itself, and this duty had been only partially performed in fifteen of the thirty-four counties, and altogether omitted in the other nineteen. The party of Slave Labor insisted on payment of taxes as a condition of suffrage. The Free Labor party deemed the whole proceeding void, by reason of the usurpation practiced, and of the defective arrangements for the election. They discovered a design to surprise in the refusal of any guaranty that the Constitution, when framed, should be submitted to the people, for their acceptance or rejection, preparatory to an application under it for the admission of Kansas into the Union. The Governor, drawing from the ample treasury of the Executive at his command, made due exhibitions of the army, and threatened the people with an acceptance of the Lecompton Constitution, however obnoxious to them, if they should refuse to vote. With these menaces, he judiciously mingled promises of fabulous quantities of land for the endowment of roads and education. He dispensed with the test oaths and taxes, lamented the defects of census and registry, and promised the rejection of the Constitution, by himself, by the President, and by Congress, if a full, fair, and complete submission of the Constitution should not be made by the Convention; and he obtained and published pledges of such submission by the party conventions which nominated the candidates for delegates, and even by an imposing number of those candidates themselves. The people stood aloof, and refused to vote. The army protected the polls. The Slave Labor party alone voted, and voted without legal restraint, and so achieved an easy formal success by casting some two thousand ballots.

Just in this conjuncture, however, the term of three years' service which the usurping Legislature had fixed for its own members expired, and elections, authorized by itself, were to be held, for the choice, not only of new members, but of a Delegate to Congress. While the Lecompton Convention was assembling, the Free Labor party determined to attend these Territorial elections, and contest, through them, for self-government within the Territory. They put candidates in nomination, on the express ground of repudiation of the whole Lecompton proceeding. The Lecompton Convention prudently adjourned to a day beyond the elections. The parties contended at the ballot-boxes, and the result was a complete and conclusive triumph of the Free Labor party. For a moment, this victory, so important, was jeoparded by the fraudulent presentation of spurious and fabricated returns of elections in almost uninhabited districts, sufficient to transfer the triumph to the Slave Labor party, and the Free State party was proceeding to vindicate it by force. The Governor and Secretary detected, proved, and exposed, this atrocious fraud. The Lecompton Convention denounced them, and complaints against them poured in upon the President, from the slaveholding States. They were doomed from that time. The President was silent. The Lecompton Convention proceeded, and framed a Constitution which declares Slavery perpetual and irreversible, and postpones any alteration of its own provisions until after 1864, by which time they hoped that Slavery might have gained too deep a hold in the soil of Kansas to be in danger of being uprooted. All this was easy; but now came the question whether the Constitution should be submitted to the people. It was confessed that it was obnoxious to them, and, if submitted, would be rejected with indignation and contempt. An official emissary from Washington is supposed to have suggested the solution which was adopted. This was a submission in form, but not in fact. The President of the Convention, without any laws to preserve the purity of the franchise by penalties for its violation, was authorized to designate his own agents, altogether irrespectively of the Territorial authorities, and with their aid to hold an election, in which there should be no vote allowed or received, if against the Constitution itself. Each voter was permitted to cast a ballot "for the Constitution with Slavery," or "for the Constitution with no Slavery;" and it was further provided, that the Constitution should stand entire, if a majority of votes should be cast for the Constitution with Slavery, while, on the other hand, if the majority of votes cast should be "for the Constitution with no Slavery," then the existing Slavery should not be disturbed, but should remain, with its continuance, by the succession of its unhappy victims by descent forever. But even this miserable shadow of a choice between forms of a slave State Constitution was made to depend on the taking of a test oath to support and maintain it in the form which should be preferred by the majority of those who should vote on complying with that humiliation. The Governor saw that by conniving at this pitiful and wicked juggle he should both shipwreck his fame and become responsible for civil war. He remonstrated, and appealed to his chief, the President of the United States, to condemn it. Denunciations followed him from the Lecompton party within the Territory, and denunciations no less violent from the slave States were his greeting at the National Capital. The President disappointed his most effective friend and wisest counsellor. This present Congress had now assembled. The President, as if fearful of delay, forestalled our attention with recommendations to overlook the manifest objections to the transaction, and to regard the anticipated result of this mock election, then not yet held, as equivalent to an acceptance of the Constitution by the people of Kansas, alleging that the refusal of the people to vote either the ballot for the "Constitution with Slavery," or the false and deceitful ballot for the "Constitution with no Slavery," would justly be regarded as drawing after it the consequences of actual acceptance and adoption of the Constitution itself. His argument was apologetic, as it lamented that the Constitution had not been fairly submitted; and jesuitical, as it urged that the people might, when once admitted as a State, change the Constitution at their pleasure, in defiance of the provision which postpones any change seven years.

Copies of the message containing these arguments were transmitted to the Territory, to confound and dishearten the Free State party, and obtain a surrender, at the election to be held on the 21st of December, on the questions submitted by the Convention. The people, however, were neither misled nor intimidated. Alarmed by this act of connivance by the President of the United States with their oppressors, they began to prepare for the last arbitrament of nations. The Secretary, Mr. Stanton, now Governor *ad interim*, issued his proclamation, calling the new Territorial Legislature to assemble to provide for preserving the public peace. An Executive spy dispatched information of this proceeding to the President by telegraph, and instantly Mr. Stanton ceased to be Secretary and Governor *ad interim*, being removed by the President, by and with the advice and consent of the Senate of the United States. Thus the service of Frederick P. Stanton came to an abrupt end, but in a manner most honorable to himself. His chief, Mr. Walker, was less wise and less fortunate. He resigned. Pætus Thrasea (we are informed by Tacitus) had been often present in the Senate, when the fathers descended to unworthy acts, and did not rise in opposition; but on the occasion when Nero procured from them a decree to celebrate, as a festival, the day on which he had murdered his mother, Agrippina, Pætus left his seat, and walked out of the chamber—thus by his virtue provoking future vengeance, and yet doing no service to the cause of Liberty. Possibly Robert J. Walker may find a less stern historian.

The new Secretary, Mr. Denver, became Governor of Kansas, the fifth incumbent of that office appointed within less than four years, the legal term of one. Happily, however, for the honor of the country, three of the recalls were made on the ground of the virtues of the parties disgraced. The Pro-Consuls of the Roman provinces were brought back to the Capital to answer for their crimes.

The proceeding which the late Secretary Stanton had so wisely instituted, nevertheless, went on; and it has become, as I trust, the principal means of rescuing from tyranny the people whom he governed so briefly and yet so well. The Lecompton Constitution had directed, that on the 4th of January elections should be held to fill the State offices and the offices of members of the Legislature and member of Congress, to assume their trusts when the new State should be admitted into the Union. The Legislature of the Territory now enacted salutary laws for preserving the purity of elections in all cases. It directed the Lecompton Constitution to be submitted to a fair vote on that day, the ballots being made to express a consent to the Constitution, or a rejection of it, with or without Slavery. The Free Labor party debated anxiously on the question, whether, besides voting against that Constitution, they should, under protest, vote also for officers to assume the trusts created by it, if Congress should admit the State under it. After a majority had decided that no such votes should be cast, a minority hastily rejected the decision, and nominated candidates for those places, to be supported under protest. The success of the movement, made under the most serious disadvantages, is conclusive evidence of their strength. While the election held on the 21st of December, allowing all fraudulent votes, showed some six thousand majority for the Constitution with Slavery, over some five hundred votes for the Constitution without Slavery, the election on the 4th of January showed an aggregate majority of eleven thousand against the Constitution itself in any form, with the choice, under protest, of a Representative in Congress, and of a large majority of all the candidates nominated by the Free Labor party for the various Executive and Legislative trusts under the Lecompton Constitution.

The Territorial Legislature has abolished Slavery by a law to take effect in March, 1858, though the Lecompton Constitution contains provisions anticipating, and designed to defeat, this great act of justice and humanity. It has organized a militia, which stands ready for the defence of the rights of the people against any power. The President of the Lecompton Convention has fled the Territory, charged with an attempt to procure fraudulent returns to reverse the already declared results of the last election, and he holds the public in suspense as to his success until after his arrival at the Capital, and the decision of Congress on the acceptance of the Lecompton Constitution. In the mean time, the Territorial Legislature has called a Convention, subject to the popular approval, to be held in March next, and to form a Constitution to be submitted to the people, and, when adopted, to be the organic law of the new State of Kansas, subject to her admission into the Union. The President of the United States, having received the Lecompton Constitution, has submitted it to Congress, and insisting that the vote taken on the juggle of the Lecompton Convention, held on the 21st of December, is legally conclusive of its acceptance by the people, and absolute against the fair, direct, and unimpeachable rejection of it by that people, made on the 4th of January last, he recommends and urges and implores the admission of Kansas as a State into the Federal Union, under that false, pretended, and spurious Constitution. I refrain from any examination of this extraordinary message. My recital is less complete than I have hoped, if it does not overthrow all the President's arguments in favor of the acceptance of the Lecompton Constitution as an act of the people of Kansas, however specious, and without descending to any details. In Congress, those who seek the admission of Kansas under that Constitution, strive to delay the admission of Minnesota, until their opponents shall compromise on that paramount question.

This, Mr. President, is a concise account of the national intervention in the Territories in favor of slave labor and slave States since 1820. No wonder that the question before us excites apprehensions and alarms. There is at last a North side of this Chamber, a North side of the Chamber of Representatives, a North side of the Union, as well as South sides of all these. Each of them is watchful, jealous, and resolute. If it be true, as has so often been asserted, that this Union cannot survive the decision by Congress of a direct question involving the adoption of a free State which will establish the ascendency of free States under the Constitution, and draw after it the restoration of the influence of Freedom in the domestic and foreign conduct of the Government, then the day of dissolution is at hand.

I have thus, Mr. President, arrived at the third circumstance attending the Kansas question which I have thought worthy of consideration, namely, that the national intervention in the Territories in favor of slave labor and slave States is opposed to the material, moral, and social developments of the Republic. The proposition seems to involve a paradox, but it is easy to understand that the checks which the Constitution applies, through prudent caution, to the relative increase of the representation of the free States in the House of Representatives, and especially in the Senate, co-operating with the differences of temper and political activity between the two classes of States, may direct the Government of the Federal Union in one course, while the tendencies of the nation itself, popularly regarded, are in a direction exactly opposite.

The ease and success which attended the earlier policy of intervention in favor of free labor and free States, and the resistance which the converse policy of intervention in favor of slave labor and slave States encounters, sufficiently establish the existence of the antagonism between the Government and the nation which I have asserted. A vessel moves quietly and peacefully while it descends with the current. You mark its way by the foam on its track only when it is forced against the tide. I will not dwell on other proofs—such as the more rapid growth of the free States, the ruptures of ecclesiastical Federal Unions, and the demoralization and disorganization of political parties.

Mr. President, I have shown why it is that the Kansas question is attended by difficulties and dangers only by way of preparation for the submission of my opinions in regard to the manner in which that question ought to be determined and settled. I think, with great deference to the judgments of others, that the expedient, peaceful, and right way to determine it, is to reverse the existing policy of intervention in favor of slave labor and slave States. It would be wise to restore the Missouri prohibition of Slavery in Kansas and Nebraska. There was peace in the Territories and in the States until that great statute of Freedom was subverted. It is true that there were frequent debates here on the subject of Slavery, and that there were profound sympathies among the people, awakened by or responding to those debates. But what was Congress instituted for but debate? What makes the American people to differ from all other nations, but this—that while among them power enforces silence, here all public questions are referred to debate, free debate in Congress. Do you tell me that the Supreme Court of the United States has removed the foundations of that great statute? I reply, that they have done no such thing; they could not do it. They have remanded the negro man Dred Scott to the custody of his master. With that decree we have nothing here, at least nothing now, to do. This is the extent of the judgment rendered, the extent of any judgment they could render. Already the pretended further decision is subverted in Kansas. So it will be in every free State and in every free Territory of the United States. The Supreme Court, also, can reverse its spurious judgment more easily than we could reconcile the people to its usurpation. Sir, the Supreme Court of the United States attempts to command the people of the United States to accept the principles that one man can own other men, and that they must guaranty the inviolability of that false and pernicious property. The people of the United States never can, and they never will, accept principles so unconstitutional and so abhorrent. Never, never. Let the Court recede. Whether it recede or not, we shall reorganize the Court, and thus reform its political sentiments and practices, and bring them into harmony with the Constitution and with the laws of nature. In doing so, we shall not only reassume our own just authority, but we shall restore that high tribunal itself to the position it ought to maintain, since so many invaluable rights of citizens, and even of States themselves, depend upon its impartiality and its wisdom.

Do you tell me that the slave States will not acquiesce, but will agitate? Think first whether the free States will acquiesce in a decision that shall not only be unjust, but fraudulent. True, they will not menace the Republic. They have an easy and simple remedy, namely, to take the Government out of unjust and unfaithful hands, and commit it to those which will be just and faithful. They are ready to do this now. They want only a little more harmony of purpose and a little more completeness of organization. These will result from only the least addition to the pressure of Slavery upon them. You are lending all that is necessary, and even more, in this very act. But will the slave States agitate? Why? Because they have lost at last a battle that they could not win, unwisely provoked, fought with all the advantages of strategy and intervention, and on a field chosen by themselves. What would they gain? Can they compel Kansas to adopt Slavery against her will? Would it be reasonable or just to do it, if they could? Was negro servitude ever forced by the sword on any people that inherited the blood which circulates in our veins, and the sentiments which make us a free people? If they will agitate on such a ground as this, then how, or when, by what concessions we can make, will they ever be satisfied? To what end would they agitate? It can now be only to divide the Union. Will they not need some fairer or more plausible excuse for a proposition so desperate? How would they improve their condition, by drawing down a certain ruin upon themselves? Would they gain any new security for Slavery? Would they not hazard securities that are invaluable? Sir, they who talk so idly, talk what they do not know themselves. No man when cool can promise what he will do when he shall be inflamed; no man inflamed can speak for his actions when time and necessity shall bring reflection. Much less can any one speak for States in such emergencies.

But, I shall not insist, now, on so radical a measure as the restoration of the Missouri prohibition. I know how difficult it is for power to relinquish even a pernicious and suicidal policy all at once. We may attain the same result, in this particular case of Kansas, without going back so far. Go back only to the ground assumed in 1854, the ground of popular sovereignty. Happily for the authors of that measure, the zealous and energetic resistance of abuses practiced under it has so far been effective that popular sovereignty in Kansas may now be made a fact, and Liberty there may be rescued from danger through its free exercise. Popular sovereignty is an epic of two parts. Part the first presents Freedom in Kansas lost. Part the second, if you will so consent to write it, shall be Freedom in Kansas regained. It is on this ground that I hail the eminent Senator from Illinois [Mr. DOUGLAS] and his associates, the distinguished Senator from Michigan, [Mr. STUART,] and the youthful, but most brave Senator from California, [Mr. BRODERICK.] The late Mr. Clay told us that Providence has many ways for saving nations. God forbid that I should consent to see Freedom wounded, because my own lead or even my own agency in saving it should be rejected. I will cheerfully co-operate with these new defenders of this sacred cause in Kansas, and I will award them all due praise, when we shall have been successful, for their large share of merit in its deliverance.

Will you tell me that it is difficult to induce the Senate and the House of Representatives to take that short backward step? On the contrary, the hardest task that an Executive dictator ever set, or parliamentary manager ever undertook, is to prevent this very step from being taken. Let the President take off his hand, and the bow, bent so long, and held to its tension by so hard a pressure, will relax, and straighten itself at once.

Consider now, if you please, the consequences of your refusal. If you attempt to coerce Kansas into the Union, under the Lecompton Constitution, the people of that Territory will resort to civil war. You are pledged to put down that revolution by the sword. Will the people listen to your voice amid the thunders of your cannon? Let but one drop of the blood of a free citizen be shed there, by the Federal army, and the countenance of every representative of a free State, in either House of Congress, will blanch, and his tongue will refuse to utter the vote necessary to sustain the army in the butchery of his fellow-citizens.

Practically, you have already one intestine and Territorial war. A war against Brigham Young in Utah. Can you carry on two, and confine the strife within the Territories? Can you win both? A wise nation will never provoke more than one enemy at one time. I know that you argue that the Free State men of Kansas are impracticable, factious, seditious? Answer me three questions: Are they not a majority, and so proclaimed by the people of Kansas? Is not this quarrel, for the right of governing themselves, conceded by the Federal Constitution? Is the tyranny of forcing a hateful Government upon them, less intolerable than three cents impost on a pound of tea, or five cents stamp duty on a promissory note? You say that they can change this Lecompton Constitution when it shall once have been forced upon them. Let it be abandoned now. What guaranty can you give against your own intervention to prevent that future change? What security can you give for your own adherence to the construction of the Constitution which you adopt, from expediency, to-day? What better is a Constitution than a by-law of a corporation, if it may be forced on a State to-day, and rejected to-morrow, in derogation of its own express inhibition?

I perceive, Mr. President, that, in the way of argument, I have passed already from the ground of expediency, on which I was standing, to that of right and justice. Among all our refinements of constitutional learning, one principle, one fundamental principle, has been faithfully preserved, namely: That the new States must come voluntarily into the Union; they must not be forced into it. "Unite or Die," was the motto addressed to the States in the time of the Revolution. Though Kansas should perish, she cannot be brought into the Union by force.

So long as the States shall come in by free consent, their admission will be an act of union, and this will be a Confederacy. Whenever they shall be brought in by fraud or force, their admission will be an act of consolidation, and the nation, ceasing to be a Confederacy, will become in reality an Empire. All our elementary instruction is wrong, or else this change of the Constitution will subvert the liberties of the American people.

You argue the consent of Kansas from documentary proofs, from her forced and partial acquiescence, under your tyrannical rule, from elections fraudulently conducted, from her own contumacy, and from your own records, made up here against her. I answer the whole argument at once: Kansas protests here, and stands, by your own confession, in an attitude of rebellion at home, to resist the annexation which you contend she is soliciting at your hands.

Sir, if your proofs were a thousand times stronger, I would not hold the people of Kansas bound by them. They all are contradicted by stern fact. A people can be bound by no action conducted in their name, and pretending to their sanction, unless they enjoy perfect freedom and safety in giving that consent. You have held the people of Kansas in duress from the first hour of their attempted organization as a community. To crown this duress by an act, at once forcing Slavery on them, which they hate, and them into a union with you, on terms which they abhor, would be but to illustrate anew, and on a grand scale, the maxim—

"*Prosperum et felix scelus, virtus vocatur.*"

Mr. President, it is an occasion for joy and triumph, when a community that has gathered itself together under circumstances of privation and exile, and proceeded through a season of Territorial or provincial dependence on distant central authority, becomes a State, in the full enjoyment of civil and religious liberty, and rises into the dignity of a member of this Imperial Union. But, in the case of Kansas, her whole existence has been, and it yet is, a trial, a tempest, a chaos—and now you propose to make her nuptials a celebration of the funeral of her freedom. The people of Kansas are entitled to save that freedom, for they have won it back when it had been wrested from them by invasion and usurpation. Sir, you are great and strong. On this continent there is no Power can resist you. On any other, there is hardly a Power that would not reluctantly engage with you—but you can never, never conquer Kansas. Your power, like a throne which is built of pine boards, and covered with purple, is weakness, except it be defended by a people confiding in you, because satisfied that you are just, and grateful for the freedom that, under you, they enjoy.

Sir, in view, once more, of this subject of Slavery, I submit that our own dignity requires that we shall give over this champerty with slaveholders, which we practice in prescribing acquiescence in their rule as a condition of toleration of self-government in the Territories. We are defeated in it. We may wisely give it up, and admit Kansas as a free State, since she will consent to be admitted only in that character.

Mr. President, if I could at all suppose it desirable or expedient to enlarge the field of slave labor, and of slaveholding sway, in this Republic, I should nevertheless maintain that it is wise to relinquish the effort to sustain Slavery in Kansas. The question, in regard to that Territory, has risen from a private one about Slavery as a domestic institution, to one of Slavery as a national policy. At every step, you have been failing. Will you go on still further, ever confident, and yet ever unsuccessful?

I believe, sir, to some extent, in the isothermal theory. I think there are regions, beginning at the North pole, and stretching southward, where Slavery will die out soon, if it be planted; and I know, too well, that in the tropics, and to some extent northward of them, Slavery lives long, and is hard to extirpate. But I cannot find a certain boundary. I am sure, however, that 36° 30′ is too far north. I think it is a movable boundary, and that every year it advances towards a more southern parallel.

But is there just now a real want of a new State for the employment of slave labor? I see and feel the need of room for a new State to be assigned to free labor, of room for such a new State almost every year. I think I see how it arises. Free white men abound in this country, and in Europe, and even in Asia. Economically speaking, their labor is cheap—there is a surplus of it. Under improved conditions of society, life grows longer, and men multiply faster. Wars, which sometimes waste them, grow less frequent and less destructive. Invention is continually producing machines and engines, artificial laborers, crowding them from one field of industry to another—ever more from the Eastern regions of this continent to the West, ever more from the overcrowded Eastern continent to the prairies and the wildernesses in our own. But I do not see any such overflowing of the African slave population in this country, even where it is unresisted. Free labor has been obstructed in Kansas. There are, nevertheless, 50,000 or 60,000 freemen gathered there already; gathered there within four years. Slave labor has been free to importation. There are only 100 to 200 slaves there. To settle and occupy a new slave State anywhere is, *pari passu*, to depopulate old slave States. Whence, then, are the supplies of slaves to come, and how? Only by reviving the African slave trade. But this is forbidden. Visionaries dream that the prohibition can be repealed. The idea is insane. A Republic of thirty millions of freemen, with a free white laboring population so dense as already to crowd on subsistence, to be brought to import negroes from Africa to supplant them as cultivators, and so to subject themselves to starvation Though Africa is yet unorganized, and unable to protect itself, still it has already exchanged, in a large degree, its wars to make slaves, and its commerce in slaves, for legitimate agriculture and trade. All European States are interested in the civilization of that continent, and they will not consent that we shall arrest it. The Christian church cannot be forced back two centuries, and be made to sanction the African slave trade as a missionary enterprise.

Every nation has always some ruling idea, which, however, changes with the several stages of its development. A ruling idea of the colonies on this continent, two hundred years ago, was labor to subdue and reclaim nature. Then African Slavery was seized and employed as an auxiliary, under a seeming necessity. That idea has ceased forever. It has given place to a new one. Aggrandizement of the nation, not indeed as it once was, to make a small State great, but to make a State already great the greatest of all States. It still demands labor, but it is no longer the ignorant labor of barbarians, but labor perfected by knowledge and skill, and combination with all the scientific principles of mechanism. It demands, not the labor of slaves, which needs to be watched and defended, but voluntary, enlightened labor, stimulated by interest, affection, and ambition. It needs that every man shall own the land he tills; that every head shall be fit for the helmet, and every hand fit for the sword, and every mind ready and qualified for counsel. To attempt to aggrandize a country with slaves for its inhabitants, would be to try to make a large body of empire with feeble sinews and empty veins.

Mr. President, the expansion of territory to make slave States will only fail to be a great crime, because it is impracticable, and therefore will turn out to be a stupendous imbecility. A free republican Government, like this, notwithstanding all its constitutional checks, cannot long resist and counteract the progress of society. Slavery, wherever and whenever, and in whatsoever form it exists, is exceptional, local, and short-lived. Freedom is the common right, interest, and ultimate destiny, of all mankind. All other nations have already abolished, or are about abolishing, Slavery. Does this fact mean nothing? All parties in this country that have tolerated the extension of Slavery, except one, has perished for that error already. That last one—the Democratic party—is hurrying on, irretrievably, toward the same fate. All Administrations that have avowed this policy have gone down dishonored for that cause, except the present one. A pit deeper and darker still is opening to receive this Administration, because it sins more deeply than its predecessors. There is a meaning in all these facts, which it becomes us to study well. The nation has advanced another stage; it has reached the point where intervention, by the Government, for Slavery and slave States, will no longer be tolerated. Free labor has at last apprehended its rights, its interests, its power, and its destiny, and is organizing itself to assume the government of the Republic. It will henceforth meet you boldly and resolutely here; it will meet you everywhere, in the Territories or out of them, wherever you may go to extend Slavery. It has driven you back in California and in Kansas; it will invade you soon in Delaware, Maryland, Virginia, Missouri, and Texas. It will meet you in Arizona, in Central America, and even in Cuba. The invasion will be not merely harmless, but beneficent, if you yield seasonably to its just and moderated demands. It proved so in New York, New Jersey, Pennsylvania, and the other slave States, which have already yielded in that way to its advances. You may, indeed, get a start under or near the tropics, and seem safe for a time, but it will be only a short time. Even there you will found States only for free labor to maintain and occupy. The interest of the white races demands the ultimate emancipation of all men. Whether that consummation shall be allowed to take effect, with needful and wise precautions against sudden change and disaster, or be hurried on by violence, is all that remains for you to decide. For the failure of your system of slave labor throughout the Republic, the responsibility will rest not on the agitators you condemn, or on the political parties you arraign, or even altogether on yourselves, but it will be due to the inherent error of the system itself, and to the error which thrusts it forward to oppose and resist the destiny, not more of the African than that of the white races. The white man needs this continent to labor upon. His head is clear, his arm is strong, and his necessities are fixed. He must and will have it. To secure it, he will oblige the Government of the United States to abandon intervention in favor of slave labor and slave States, and go backward forty years, and resume the original policy of intervention in favor of free labor and free States. The fall of the castle of San Juan d'Ulloa determined the fate of Mexico, although sore sieges and severe pitched battles intervened before the capture of the capital of the Aztecs. The defeats you have encountered in California and in Kansas determine the fate of the principle for which you have been contending. It is for yourselves, not for us, to decide how long and through what further mortifications and disasters the contest shall be protracted, before Freedom shall enjoy her already assured triumph. I would have it ended now, and would have the wounds of society bound up and healed. But this can be done only in one way. It cannot be done by offering further resistance, nor by any evasion or partial surrender, nor by forcing Kansas into the Union as a slave State, against her will, leaving her to cast off Slavery afterwards, as she best may; nor by compelling Minnesota and Oregon to wait, and wear the humiliating costume of Territories at the doors of Congress, until the people of Kansas, or their true defenders here, shall be brought to dishonorable compromises. It can be done only by the simple and direct admission of the three new States as free States, without qualification, condition, reservation, or compromise, and by the abandonment of all further attempts to extend Slavery under the Federal Constitution. You have unwisely pushed the controversy so far, that only these broad concessions will now be accepted by the interest of free labor and free States. For myself, I see this fact, perhaps, the more distinctly now, because I have so long foreseen it. I can therefore counsel nothing less than those concessions. I know the hazards I incur in taking this position. I know how men and parties, now earnest, and zealous, and bold, may yet fall away from me, as the controversy shall wax warm, and alarms and dangers, now unlooked for, shall stare them in the face, as men and parties, equally earnest, bold, and zealous, have done, in like circumstances, before. But it is the same position I took in the case of California, eight years ago. It is the same I maintained on the great occasion of the organization of Kansas and Nebraska, four years ago. Time and added experience have vindicated it since, and I assume it again, to be maintained to the last, with confidence, that it will be justified, ultimately, by the country and by the civilized world. You may refuse to yield it now, and for a short period, but your refusal will only animate the friends of Freedom with the courage and the resolution, and produce the union among them, which alone are necessary, on their part, to attain the position itself simultaneously with the impending overthrow of the existing Federal Administration and the constitution of a new and more independent Congress.

Mr. President, this expansion of the empire of free white men is to be conducted through the process of admitting new States, and not otherwise. The white man, whether you consent or not, will make the States to be admitted, and he will make them all free States. We must admit them, and admit them all free; otherwise, they will become independent and foreign States, constituting a new empire to contend with us for the continent. To admit them is a simple, easy, and natural policy. It is not new to us, or to our times. It began with the voluntary union of the first thirteen. It has continued to go on, overriding all resistance, ever since. It will go on until the ends of the continent are the borders of our Union. Thus we become co-laborers with our fathers, and even with our posterity throughout many ages. After times, contemplating the whole vast structure, completed and perfected, will forget the dates, and the eras, and the individualities, of the builders in their successive generations. It will be one great Republic, founded by one body of benefactors. I wonder that the President of the United States undervalues the Kansas question, when it is a part of a transaction so immense and sublime. Far from sympathizing with him in his desire to depreciate it, and to be rid of it, I felicitate myself on my humble relation to it, for I know that Heaven cannot grant nor man desire a more favorable occasion to acquire fame, than he enjoys who is engaged in laying the foundations of a great empire; and I know, also, that while mankind have often deified their benefactors, no nation has ever yet bestowed honors on the memories of the founders of Slavery.

I have always believed, Mr. President, that

this glorious Federal Constitution of ours is adapted to the inevitable expansion of the empire which I have so feebly presented. It has been perverted often by misconstruction, and it has yet to be perverted many times, and widely, hereafter; but it has inherent strength and vigor that will cast off all the webs which the ever-changing interests of classes may weave around it. If it fail us now, it will, however, not be our fault, but because an inevitable crisis, like that of youth, or of manhood, is to be encountered by a constitution proved in that case to be inadequate to the trial. I am sure that no patriot, who views the subject as I do, could wish to evade or delay the trial. By delay we could only extend Slavery, at the most, throughout the Atlantic region of the continent. The Pacific slope is free, and it always must and will be free. The mountain barriers that separate us from that portion of our empire are quite enough to alienate us too widely, possibly to separate us too soon. Let us only become all slave-holding States on this side of those barriers, while only free States are organized and perpetuated on the other side, and then indeed there will come a division of the great American family into two nations, equally ambitious for complete control over the continent, and a conflict between them, over which the world will mourn, as the greatest and last to be retrieved of all the calamities that have ever befallen the human race.

www.ingramcontent.com/pod-product-compliance
Lightning Source LLC
LaVergne TN
LVHW020639110826
845149LV00004B/1292